Flashes of Brightness

More reflections on the journey
from the author of
Candles and Kingfishers

Ann Lewin

ISBN 1 85852 202 1

© 2001 Trustees for Methodist Church Purposes
First published 2001
This edition 2002

Printed by Stanley L Hunt (Printers) Ltd, Rushden

PREFACE

> *. . . sometimes, when you've almost*
> *Stopped expecting it,*
> *A flash of brightness*
> *Gives encouragement.*

That quotation, from 'Disclosure', in *Candles and Kingfishers* (my earlier book of poetry) provides a link between that volume and this. The flashes of insight that come as we ponder prayerfully on what is happening in our lives or in the world around us, or on passages of scripture, are always a gift. And gifts are to be shared.

As with previous publications, I offer my reflections to my fellow pilgrims, with the prayer that they will be helpful on your journey.

Ann Lewin
55 Crabwood Road
Maybush
Southampton
SO16 9FB

ENTRANCE

Pause at the threshold
Of the sacred space;
Bow low.
Prepare for fresh
Encounter
With the Holy One.

STAGE FRIGHT

It's often somewhat
Disconcerting when
God takes us at our word.
'Take me and use me,'
We say, meaning it;
But when God does,
There is a moment of surprise,
Perhaps terror, 'Me'?

Then, our 'Yes' loved from us,
Comes the realisation
That the opportunity is gift,
The outcome held in grace.

Moving Mountains

Only have faith . . .
But that's the problem;
How much do we need?
What if we haven't enough?

The questions miss the point:
Faith is not a commodity
To be possessed,
A bargaining counter
Used to get things done;
Faith is the orientation
Of our lives, a gift
Which shifts perceptions,
Takes us deeper
Into the mystery of God.

CHALLENGE

On that night, there were
Two bowls of water.

The first was taken
And used for washing feet,
Symbol, he said, of love.

The second was called for
And used for washing hands,
Disclaiming responsibility.

The bowls are constantly before us:
Into which will we dip our hands?

CHRISTMAS CARD

The figures are the same:
The tender curves of
A mother cradling her child.
But there is no breastful of milk
To satisfy this infant
Whose cries of hunger echo her own.
Their eyes look blankly
At a world which offers little hope.

Come on, ye faithful,
And all people of goodwill,
It is time to be midwives
For the love of God
Struggling again to birth;
Deliver healing
To our crying world.

REFUGEES

They stream across our screens
Balancing impossible burdens;
The remnants of their lives
Tied up in bundles.
Yet what we see is nothing
To the burdens they carry
In their hearts:
Loss, pain and fear.

Asylum seekers

They live under the shadow of
A two-edged sword: in a place of safety
And a state of fear. The rules
Ensure *we* are kept safe; *our* fear
Defines our hospitality,
Keeps them on edge.
Compassion is constrained
By prudent care.

Could we, instead of seeing problems,
Begin to recognise the gifts they bring,
And be enriched by their humanity?

Lighten our darkness

When I was a child,
They were killing children
And I didn't know;
Men and women too,
Led to the gas chambers
By people who were
Only obeying orders.

Now I am grown, aware;
It happens still, not always
By deliberate act –
A terrible carelessness
Corrupts our use of power,
Lets people be expendable.

I can't blame 'them';
Like everyone, I have within
A place of guilt and shame
Like Auschwitz, where
It's always night.

With you, Lord,
Darkness is light.
Strengthen your light in us
Until it snuffs out darkness.

Elie Wiesel, an Auschwitz survivor, speaking at a ceremony commemorating the fiftieth anniversary of the discoveries at Auschwitz said, 'Here it is always night.' People at that ceremony lit candles and placed them on the railway tracks leading to the gas chambers. The event coincided with Candlemas.

For My Salvation?

A shaft of light caught the crucifix in the chapel in Burford Priory, and started a train of thought . . .

His bloodied knees
Caught my attention . . .
I've grown accustomed
To the sight of blood
Pouring from thorn-crowned head
And marks of nails and spear:
The crucified Christ
Bearing the sins of the world.
A distant Christ, carrying
The big sins – murder,
Premeditated cruelty –
Other people's sins, not often mine.
(Although I have it in me.)

But the sore knees
Brought him close.
That blood comes from
Everyone's experience;
Tripped up by inattention,
Undue haste, or thoughtlessness,
We feel the sting.
Those sins I know,
Catching me unaware.

It was the weight of such sins
Caused him to fall under the cross
And graze his knees.

Should I not then cry, Mercy?

The next four poems were written in response to the experience of having breast cancer.

Unwelcome Visitor

A needle in my breast,
A word, *malignant*,
And a sword pierced my soul.

Crabbed insidiousness,
Who gave you leave
To enter and attempt
Possession?
Don't get too comfortable,
You are not welcome.
Eviction follows swiftly
On this notice.

Marked for life

Ash Wednesday, cross-shaped mark
Remember you are dust . . .
A touch that brands and heals,
The mark, like Cain's a sign of
God's protection.

And now, another
Reminder of mortality:
Lines drawn for radiotherapy.
Could these too be
A sign of God's protection,
Focusing healing rays
Not coming gently
But with searing power?

Come, Holy Spirit,
Come in these rays
To cleanse and heal.

DARK MOMENTS

'All shall be well' . . .
She* must have said that
Sometimes through gritted teeth.
Surely she knew the moments
When fear gnaws at trust,
The future loses shape,
Gethsemane?

The courage that says
'All shall be well'
Doesn't mean feeling no fear,
But facing it, trusting
God won't let go.

'All shall be well'
Doesn't deny present experience,
But roots it deep
In the faithfulness of God,
Whose will and gift is life.

* Julian of Norwich

VULNERABLE

We've been here before, Lord,
You and I. A situation
Not of your will, and
Certainly not my choice.
I can't believe that you send
Suffering, and I don't want it.
We look at each other,
And feel the pain
That this is how it is.

I do not acquiesce
Without complaint;
And yet the words die on my lips,
For in response you come
With wounded hands
And cradle me in love.

COMPASSION

Suffering, sharing
The pain;
Knowing within oneself
Some of the cost.
Spurred to activity,
One hand stretched out
To those who suffer,
One stretched out to
God who suffers too.
Nothing sentimental:
The sharp edge of love,
Like crucifixion.

BEREAVEMENT

Dark place
Where, vulnerable, alone,
We lick the wounds of loss.

Wise friends say little,
But hold us in their love,
And listen.

There are no guarantees,
Only reports from those
Who've been there,
That there is hope,
And life persists.

TOMB

The place of remembering:
Where, as the work of grief is done,
Memory recovers its perspective.

Letting the dead one go,
With aching sense of loss,
Opens the way to finding again
A rounded person, gifts and faults
Delights and irritations;
Makes it possible to share again
The jokes, the intimate glance,
Keep company unseen.

RESURRECTION

There are times when,
All being darkness and loss,
There is nothing for it
But to pick up your cross
And dance with it.

PREPARATION

From sudden death,
Good Lord, deliver us.

But death is always sudden,
Slipping between one moment
And eternity. We can't escape.
Indeed, that way of death
Is what I hope for:
Not for me the painful diminishment
Of long, slow dying –
That's much more to be feared.

The trouble is, that
When death suddenly
Catches our breath
We leave loose ends,
Relationships at odds
Or words unsaid:
Fuel for guilt for those
Surviving, quite apart
From any personal
Dissatisfaction.

Perhaps our prayer should be
For more awareness;
Not preoccupation
With our mortal end,
But aliveness to
This moment's possibilities.
It may just be our last.

For sudden death,
Good Lord, prepare us.

AUTUMN

After a sharp frost, on a windless morning,
I watched leaves falling . . .

The frost has made the leaves
Lose their grip. Like pattering rain
They fall, returning to earth.

Might death be like that,
A gentle falling to the dust
From which I came?
Must I go raging into that
Dark night? Could I not,
As the sharp frost of age
Begins to chill,
Simply let go?

YEAR'S MIND

Every year, I pass the day
Not knowing. Someday
Someone will say, 'Oh yes,
Ann died a year ago.'

I pray they will remember
A day when I lived to the full,
A day of celebration
Of the gift of life.

LAST THINGS

Death

It is not death I fear, but
Dying. How will it come?
Will it be sudden, violent,
Catching me in surprise or
Indignation? Or a slow
Decline, stripping away
Control, perhaps with pain or
Loss of faculties? Those I fear.
Could I choose, I would go gently,
Full of years, to that still place
Where flesh and spirit part.
Travelling light, as when I first
Arrived, naked, to birth.

Judgement

Death is a gift, God's last,
Perhaps his greatest,
Setting us free to know him
As he is, and see ourselves
Uncluttered by our outward
Circumstance. And then,
Our motives bared before us,
Will we stand,
Looking God in the eye, gladly
Acknowledging our inmost selves?
Or will we understand at last
Why we pray, 'Lord, have mercy'?

Hell

It would be hell to find
It was a lie, this talk of
God. To meet not him, but
Emptiness. No need for
Torment, flaming fire, the
Medieval tortures:
To wake and find there's
Nothing would be Hell.

Heaven

How can our language,
Formed for time and space, express
The timeless graciousness of God?
What of ourselves, how will we be
When limits to loving are removed?
To know how we are known,
The judgement past, should fill us
Not with terror but with joy.
Complete acceptance in the love of God –
Will that be Heaven?

TERMINOLOGY

Productivity:
Forced outcome of
Endeavour;

Unlike *fruitfulness:*
Result of fallow
Darkness
When time seems wasted.

Seasons take their time:
Nothing is lost, our waiting,
Open and expectant
Leads to harvest.

What's in a Word?

Present, a mean word
To describe an offering.

Presents come from
A position of strength –
You have something to give.
An *offering* comes from
Weakness, an opening of
Yourself in vulnerability –
A handful of wilting flowers
Clutched by a child, offered
'For you.'
Always inadequate,
But received and valued.

*The last verse of When I survey the wondrous cross
has variant readings:*

Were the whole realm of nature mine,
That were ⌠a present far too small
*   ⌡an offering*
Love so amazing, so divine,
Demands my soul, my life, my all.

PERSPECTIVE

Ascension means a
God-like view of things,
Rising above our usual
Limitations.
Rise, then, and know
The glory of a life
Set free from fear.

WAIT FOR THE SPIRIT

Wait . . .
Without expectation
Which might focus
Attention too narrowly,
So that we miss the coming.

Wait with expectancy, alert,
Hearts, minds, hands, ears
Open to receive the gift.

LORD, HAVE MERCY

God, you overstepped the mark
At Pentecost. Those boundaries
So clearly drawn: be clean,
Be holy, do not dare draw near
Unless your hearts are pure,
Your sins forgiven – they kept us safe.
Then suddenly, with burning fire
And rushing wind,
You broke down our defences,
Surprised your way
Into our lives.

We're at your mercy.
Can we bear
To be that close?

ORDINARY TIME

A vellum fragment of the Rule,
Cover and outer pages long since gone;
Nothing ornate, a working document,
Stained with use as well as time.

I held it, and I thought
Of all whose hands had held it too,
People like us, who through the years
Followed the daily discipline
Of prayer, a diverse company
Seeking God's mercy.

Wells Cathedral Library is home to a fragment of the Benedictine Rule, dated around 1000 AD, probably originating at Glastonbury.

Going to Lauds

The rooks swirled in the dawn sky,
Greeting each other and the day
In noisy Benedicite.
Like thoughts in disarray,
They flew, and perched,
And flew again,
Finding, apparently, any excuse . . .
Then, just when it seemed
That all was stilled,
More birds arrived, and
Off they went in great
Cacophony, to fly and perch,
And fly again.
Eventually,
Negotiations finished,
We settled,
Precariously:
They to rookery, I to prayer.

DINNER PARTY

Simon

I'll do the decent thing,
Invite him for a meal.
I needn't make a fuss,
He should feel honoured to be
Here. No need to lavish
Courtesy on him.
Master, you're welcome,
Seat yourself, enjoy
The food and company.

Woman

How can he treat him so?
If Simon knew
What kind of man he is
He'd not dismiss him
So discourteously.
Master, with my tears,
And perfume once
Used to my shame,
I'll wash your feet
In loving gratitude.

Other guests

What's going on? That harlot
Drawing attention to herself!
She ought to know
We don't want her sort here,
Flaunting extravagant
Emotion. And he says
Her sins have been forgiven.
What's going on?

Jesus

Simon, what motivates your 'love'?
Desire to be thought well of? Or
Response in gratitude for sins
Forgiven? This woman knows.
Daughter, your faith has saved you.
Go in peace.

Shades of Despair

Pilate

If only they would stop that
Shouting, 'Caesar's friend,
You are not Caesar's friend
If you let this man go.' He's
Innocent, I find no fault, but
They insist. His life or mine, it seems.
'Not Caesar's friend' leads only to one
End. Who is this man? 'Behold him!'
'Crucify!' 'I wash my hands . . .'
'His blood on us,' they cry.
And as they lead him out,
My blood runs cold.

Judas

I thought he'd fight, I thought
He would at last admit that
I was right, the only way to
Win Messiah's cause was by the
Sword. He should have acted
When they yelled, 'Save now!'
He could have overthrown them.
I was wrong. My treacherous kiss
Condemned both him and me:
Him to a cross, and me to
Death of hope. My only course now
Is to end it all.

Peter

What have I done? I who would
Never leave him, so I said.
What have I done? I slept
When he most needed company,
Denied I knew him when he
Needed friends, ran when
They led him to a cross,
Stayed distant in his suffering.
How can I bear the memory of his look,
The love accepting me as friend?
Master, what have I done?

Restoration

Master, don't tease. You know
I am your friend. Yet still you ask,
And how can I reply?
I swore unending loyalty, and then
Three times denied, but Lord,
I am your friend. And still you press,
You are my friend, then? Lord it hurts,
But in the hurting heals:
Three times I say it, Yes, I am your friend.
And gladly I will serve as you command.

SIMON OF CYRENE

It wasn't what I'd planned –
My pilgrimage to join the Passover
Ended cross-carrying, glad
My sons weren't witness to my shame.

But the man, bleeding in pain –
His dignity impressed: no cursing,
But forgiving words absorbing cruelty.
Although I had the cross, it seemed
He had the weight, almost as though
World's pain bore down on him.
What should be memory of shame,
Stays with me as a turning point in love;
I felt compelled to go not just a mile,
But on an endless journey into life.

ALEXANDER AND RUFUS

They pressed him into carrying a cross,
And he was changed. Instead of feeling shame,
He said he'd glory always in that sign.
Impressed, we also turned, confessed Christ Lord,
And bear his mark of love.

KNOWN BY NAME

Who were you, Mary
From whom devils were cast out?
Did you disturb respectability
By washing his feet with tears,
An uninvited guest;
Or in embarrassing extravagance
Pour precious ointment on his head?
Were you notorious in your day,
Or a woman in the crowd from Magdala,
Who found new purpose
Being set free to love,
And used your gifts
In faithful ministry?

Perhaps it doesn't matter.
Perhaps, like all of us,
You were a mixture:
Damaged and healed;
Longing to be loved,
And struggling to relate;
Passionate and reserved
By turns, working out
Costly discipleship.

The important moment
Was when you heard your name,
And answered and were sent,
No longer clinging to what kept you safe,
Strong in the power of the risen Lord,
To witness to new life.

Too Busy to Pray

It must have smarted,
That implied rebuke.*
She was only doing
What hospitality required,
And they would both
Want to be fed.

But when she thought about it later,
I wonder if she realised
She too had a choice?

She could have sat with Mary at his feet
Absorbed in his teaching,
Enlarging her inner space;
Work would have waited.

Perhaps then Mary would have
Joined her in the chores,
And both discovered
The better part that
None can take away,
Their work transformed
By the presence
They had practised.

* Luke 10:38-42

No easy place

In this room, where you can see
The city through one window,
The cathedral through another
(Mary and Martha as it were, opposed)
The question comes again,
Where do we find you?

The dominant building
Makes assumptions not borne out
By experience, for
Bruised and broken people
Live in both aspects, and
Prayer is made in busy streets
As well as cathedral calm.

God, elusive, slips
Out of the fortress
Built to keep him safe, and
Wanders the streets, looking for
Allies willing to try
The steep hill of connection,
And keep him company
In work and prayer, without
Prescribing the location.

Written in Edward King House, Lincoln, in the room Bishop King referred to as the Mary and Martha room. For those who don't know Lincoln, the hill joining the cathedral and castle to the rest of the city is called, and is, Steep Hill.

Get Real

You always appear
Too good to be true, Mary.
We've pictured you always serene,
Never exasperated by a fractious child,
Apparently having no feelings.

But surely that initial *Yes* came
From a moment of overwhelming terror?
And the birth tore you to the core?
Didn't he ever cry, that baby,
Give you sleepless nights?
Didn't he irritate you,
That precocious son
Dismissing your anxiety with
Didn't you know? And later
That wounding question,
Who is my mother?
My mother would have told him . . .
Perhaps you did too,
But it wasn't recorded.

Even at the end, you're pictured
Beautiful in your sorrow,
Holding your dead child.
Not like those ravaged faces
We see on our screens
Raging at the senseless
Killing of the innocent.

What's the reality?
Is it more like the aged Madonna,
Gaunt, face lined by experience;
With hint of an arthritic hip
Walking towards the complexities of life,
Away from cloistered peace?
Her hand is polished smooth
By the touch of countless hands.

The walking Madonna by Elizabeth Frink
strides through the Close in Salisbury.

St Anne

The moment every mother dreads:
Whatever did you feel like?
Could you share it with your
Husband? Did you feel, like
Joseph, that there was no
Alternative to putting her
Away privily? Even then
There was the rest of the family,
And the neighbours were bound to talk.
The shame of it.

Gracious, your name means.
You must have been a real
Source of grace to Mary,
Supporting her through those months.
One of those people
Who make it possible
For others to cope.

MAN OF FIRE

We've turned him into someone
Who was kind to animals,
Drowned him in sentiment.

But this man was impossible:
An all or nothing man
With fire in his belly.
He gave up all, that
Nothing should
Stand in the way of
Absolute commitment.

Of course he was kind,
And full of respect for
All creation. Perhaps
He recognised in animals
His own directness.

But he was uncomfortable too;
He stripped life of
Pretensions to power,
Insisted that we should
Embrace the leper of
Our own unloveliness,
And live out love
In great simplicity.

CELTIC KNOT

The tangled roots from which I spring
Nourish my depths and
Send out shoots for growth;
Separate yet entwined
Friends, relatives, strangers
And people I don't like,
We grow together in
Intricate relationship.

Weaver God, pick up the
Threads of my experience,
Craft the pattern, and
In your time
Reveal significance.

LIFE BLESSING

Deep peace enfold you,
Encircle and hold you
In youth and in age,
At life's every stage.
At birth and in growing,
In failing and dying,
The sacred three
Your protection be.

Age Blessing

At ear close and tooth drop,
At sight fail and mind loss,
The sacred three
Enliven thee.

Lullaby

Rest in the love of the Father,
Rest in the love of the Son,
Rest in the love of the Spirit.
The love of the sacred Three
Your rest-place be.

DAYBREAK

As at the dawn of creation,
The lake awaits light's coming;
Herons stand, grey wraiths
In the swirling mist;
Wing-stretchings, stirrings in
Undergrowth, greet the day;
Questioning chirps from a
Secret world swell to
Full throat's song
In the strengthening sun;
A kingfisher – glimpse of glory
Glancing in sunlight.
No wonder God rejoices:
It is very good.

BENEDICITE

Swans came this morning,
Curving whiteness
Reflected on the lake.
They stayed, feeding,
Delighting those who saw.
Then, with that slow,
Distinctive wing beat,
They flew,
Leaving a sadness
On the empty lake.
So beautiful,
They stir strange longings.
Will they return?
We would be honoured
To be chosen for such
Privilege.

Peace Trees

To be in the presence of trees
Is to know peace.
The silent rhythm of their life,
Bringing maturity in due time,
Without anxiety or haste,
Calms our impatience;
Their solid strength, derived from
Hidden roots spreading much further
Than we ever know, gives us security;
Grace, beauty, shapeliness and form,
Delight our senses, soothe our
Fragile nerves, and bring refreshment.

Let us in turn be trees,
Growing in God's time to maturity,
Spreading our roots deep into springs of life,
Opening branches wide to all who come
Offering strength and healing through our
Peace.

MAGNIFICAT FOR THREE CHOIRS

Encircled by music,
Harmonies swirling from
Choir to answering choir,
Swelling at last to join in
High thanksgiving . . .
It was like being
Drawn into the Rublev icon.

The three conductors,
Watching each other
With courteous attention,
Drew from each choir
Sounds of great beauty,
Invited us to join
Their creativity, and
Offer our hearts
With their Magnificat.

Written after hearing the three cathedral choirs gathered in different places in Winchester Cathedral sing Victoria's Magnificat at the Southern Cathedrals Festival 1999.

Action Plan

'What will you do now?'
People asked when I retired.
'Guard the space,' I said.

Thanksgiving

Given so much,
What have I done to
Deserve it?
Nothing,
Absolutely nothing.

No wonder my heart
Dances.

INDEX

* indicates that the item appeared in one of the volumes which preceded *Candles and Kingfishers*, all now out of print